Table of Contents

Introduction

Chairman McKeon, Ranking Member Smith, and distinguished Members of the Committee: I appreciate the opportunity to appear before you today to discuss U.S. Southern Command's efforts in Central America, South America, and the Caribbean. Mr. Chairman, Members, even our significantly reduced engagement continues to yield dividends in a region of increasing importance to our national interests. While other global concerns dominate the headlines, we should not lose sight of either the challenges or opportunities closer to home. In terms of geographic proximity, trade, culture, immigration, and the environment, no other part of the world has greater impact on daily life in our country than Latin America and the Caribbean.

During my first year in command, I established four priorities for U.S. Southern Command—continuing humane and dignified detention operations at Joint Task Force Guantanamo, countering transnational organized crime, building partner capacity, and planning for contingencies—all of which I look forward to discussing with you today. I thank the Congress for recognizing U.S. Southern Command's vital role in defending our southern approaches and building enduring partnerships with the Americas. I remain concerned, however, by the impact of budget cuts on our ability to support national security interests and contribute to regional security.

Over the next ten years, the Services are reducing deployments of personnel, ships, and aircraft in the context of tightening fiscal constraints. As an economy of force Combatant Command, these reductions have a disproportionately large impact on our operations, exercises, and engagement activities. Insufficient maritime surface vessels and intelligence, surveillance, and reconnaissance platforms impair our primary mission to detect threats and defend the southern approaches to the U.S. homeland. Similarly, reductions in force allocation severely limit our security cooperation activities, the primary way we engage with and influence the region. Sequestration only exacerbated these challenges, and while its near-term effects may have been mitigated, this reprieve is temporary. As the lowest priority Geographic Combatant Command, U.S. Southern Command will likely receive little, if any, "trickle down" of restored funding. Ultimately, the cumulative impact of our reduced engagement will be measured in terms of U.S. influence, leadership, and relationships in the Western Hemisphere. Severe budget constraints have serious implications for all three, at a time in which regional security issues warrant greater attention.

Overview of Regional Security Issues

Transnational Organized Crime. Mr. Chairman, Members, transnational organized crime is a national security concern for three primary reasons. First, the spread of criminal networks is having a corrosive effect on the integrity of democratic institutions and the stability of several of our partner nations. Transnational criminal organizations threaten citizen security, undermine basic human rights, cripple rule of law through corruption, erode good governance, and hinder economic development.[1] Second, illicit trafficking poses a direct threat to our nation's public health, safety, and border security. Criminal elements make use of the multitude of illicit pathways in our hemisphere to smuggle drugs, contraband, and even humans directly into the United States. Illegal drugs are an epidemic in our country, wasting lives and fueling violence

---

[1] Director of National Intelligence, James R. Clapper. Statement for the Record: Worldwide Threat Assessment of the US Intelligence Community. Senate Select Committee on Intelligence, March 12, 2013.

between rival gangs in most of our nation's cities. The third concern is a potential one, and highlights the vulnerability to our homeland rather than an imminent threat: that terrorist organizations could seek to leverage those same smuggling routes to move operatives with intent to cause grave harm to our citizens or even quite easily bring weapons of mass destruction into the United States. I would like to briefly talk about each concern in greater detail to underscore the magnitude of the threat posed by transnational organized crime.

Destabilizing Effects in the Region. The unprecedented expansion of criminal networks and violent gangs is impacting citizen security and stability in the region. Skyrocketing criminal violence exacerbates existing challenges like weak governance; as a United Nations report recently noted, despite improvements, Latin America remains the most unequal and insecure region in the world.[2] In some countries, homicides are approaching crisis levels. High levels of violence are driving Central American citizens to seek refuge in other countries, including the United States. Driven by economic pressures and rising criminal violence, the number of Hondurans, Guatemalans, and Salvadorans attempting to cross the U.S. Southwest border increased 60 percent in 2013.[3]

This challenge, however, extends far beyond a threat to public safety; some areas of Central America are under the direct influence of drug trafficking organizations. These groups use their illegally gained wealth to buy off border agents, judges, police officers, and even entire villages. This criminal power and the enormous flow of crime-generated profits are serious threats to the stability of democratic institutions, rule of law,

---

[2] United Nations Development Programme (UNDP). Human Development Report for Latin America 2013-2014.
[3] Information provided by U.S. Customs and Border Protection.

and the international financial system. Corruption also poses an indirect threat to U.S. national security interests, as corrupt government officials in the region can be bribed to procure official documents such as visas or citizenship papers and facilitate travel of special interest aliens. In my view, this vulnerability could be exploited by any number of actors seeking to do us harm.

Illicit Trafficking to the United States. The U.S. Southern Command area of responsibility is the distribution hub for drug trafficking destined for the United States. The majority of heroin sold in the United States comes from either Colombia or Mexico, and we are seeing a significant increase in heroin-related overdoses and deaths in our country.[4] Additionally, opium poppy production now appears to be increasing in Guatemala. Thousands of tons of precursor chemicals are trafficked into our hemisphere from China, aiding Mexican-based drug cartels that are extending production of U.S.-bound methamphetamine into Guatemala, Nicaragua, and potentially other Central American countries. With an estimated $84 billion in annual global sales,[5] cocaine trafficking remains the most profitable activity for criminal networks operating in the region, as the Andean Ridge is the source of every single ounce of cocaine consumed on the planet.[6] Upon landfall in Central America, bulk cocaine is broken down into multiple smaller shipments for transit into Mexico and the United States, making large interdictions at the U.S. border extremely difficult, despite the heroic efforts of local law enforcement, U.S. Customs and Border Protection, and Immigrations and Customs Enforcement. If bulk shipments are not interdicted before making landfall, there is

---

[4] U.S. Department of Justice Drug Enforcement Administration. *2013 National Drug Threat Assessment.*
[5] United Nations Office of Drugs and Crime (UNODC). *Estimating illicit financial flows resulting from drug trafficking and other transnational organized crime,* 2011.

almost no stopping the majority of this cocaine as it moves through Central America and Mexico and eventually lands on street corners across America, placing significant strain on our nation's health care and criminal justice systems and costing American taxpayers an estimated $193 billion in 2007 alone, the most recent year for which data is available.[7,8]

Cocaine trafficking remains the predominant security challenge throughout the entire region, and I am growing increasingly concerned by the situation in the Caribbean.

According to U.S. Customs and Border Protection, there was a 483% increase in cocaine washing up on Florida's shores in 2013 compared to 2012. Due in part to counterdrug asset reductions, some old routes appear to be reviving, including ones that lead directly into Florida. In 2013, U.S.-bound cocaine flow through the Caribbean corridor increased to 14% of the overall estimated flow; this number is likely higher and will continue to grow, but we lack a clear picture of cocaine flow due to asset shortfalls. The discovery of cocaine processing lab equipment in the Dominican Republic suggests criminal organizations may be seeking to broaden production in the Caribbean. This may be an indication of an emerging trend, similar to what we saw in Central America in 2012. Additionally, the Caribbean is particularly vulnerable to the violence and insecurity that often comes with illicit trafficking and organized crime. As trafficking from the Dominican Republic into Puerto Rico has increased, so too have violence, crime, and corruption. Once cocaine successfully reaches Puerto Rico, it has reached the U.S. homeland; most of the cocaine arriving in Puerto Rico is successfully transported into the continental United States. According to

---

[7] Note: Upon landfall in Central America, bulk cocaine is broken down into multiple smaller shipments for transit into Mexico and the United States, making large interdictions extremely difficult.

[8] National Drug Intelligence Center (2011). *The Economic Impact of Illicit Drug Use on American Society.* Department of Justice.

the DEA, traffickers are also transporting Colombian heroin, often via Venezuela, to Puerto Rico for onward shipment to Miami, New York, and Houston.

Mr. Chairman, gone are the days of the "cocaine cowboys." Instead, we and our partners are confronted with cocaine corporations that have franchises all over the world, including 1,200 American cities,[9] as well as criminal enterprises like the violent transnational gang Mara Salvatrucha, or MS-13, that specialize in extortion and human trafficking. The FBI has warned that MS-13 has a significant presence in California, North Carolina, New York, and northern Virginia, and is expanding into new areas of the United States, including Indian reservations in South Dakota.

Additionally, migrant smuggling organizations are increasingly active in the Caribbean, as new laws in Cuba and erroneous perceptions in Haiti of changes in U.S. immigration policy have led to increased migration flows. Smuggling networks are expanding in the Eastern Caribbean, as Cubans and Haitians attempt to reach the United States via Puerto Rico or the U.S. Virgin Islands. These networks are opportunistic and easily expand into other illicit activities, such as the drug trade, special interest alien smuggling, and human trafficking, including exploiting vulnerable migrants by subjecting them to forced labor, a form of modern-day slavery. In 2012, the International Labor Organization estimated that 20.9 million people are victims of forced labor worldwide.[10] Foreign nationals are trafficked for sex and labor, as well as for

---

[9] U.S. Department of Justice, Drug Enforcement Administration. *2011 National Drug Threat Assessment.*
[10] ILO Global Estimate of Forced Labour, ILO. See: http://www.ilo.org/wcmsp5/groups/public/---ed_norm/---declaration/documents/publication/wcms_182004.pdf

commercial sex acts, into the United States from many countries around the world, including Central America, South America, and the Caribbean.[11]

It has been many years since U.S. Southern Command supported a response to a mass migration event, but I am concerned by the trends we are seeing, especially in Haiti, where we have witnessed a 44-fold increase in Haitian migrants in the Mona Passage. As of February 2013, more than 2,000 Haitians had been documented trying to use this narrow passage as a migration vector, compared to less than 200 in the past eight years *combined*. Smuggling operations have a high human toll; rough seas endanger the lives of rescuers and migrants and have resulted in the death of more than 50 Haitians to date. Thankfully, the Dominican Republic is an important partner in stemming migration flows, and they are working hard to reach a solution on the issue of the roughly 200,000 Haitians residing in the Dominican Republic. However, additional increases in migration would place additional burdens on already over-stretched U.S. Coast Guard and Dominican Republic assets. Absent resource adjustments, stemming these smuggling operations and preventing future loss-of-life will pose major challenges to the United States and our Caribbean partners.

Crime-Terror Convergence. Clearly, criminal networks can move just about anything on these smuggling pipelines. My concern, Mr. Chairman, is that many of these pipelines lead directly into the United States, representing a potential vulnerability that could be exploited by terrorist groups seeking to do us harm. Supporters and sympathizers of Lebanese Hezbollah are involved in both licit and illicit activities in the

---

[11] U.S. Department of State Office to Monitor and Combat Trafficking in Persons. *2013 Trafficking in Persons Report.* Retrieved from: *http://www.state.gov/documents/organization/210742.pdf.*

region, including drug trafficking. Additionally, money, like drugs and people, has become mobile; it is easier to move than ever before, and the vast global illicit economy benefits both criminal and terrorist networks alike. Clan-based, Lebanese Hezbollah-associated criminal networks exploit free trade zones and permissive areas in places like Venezuela, and the Argentina, Brazil, and Paraguay Tri-Border to engage in money laundering and other illegal endeavors, as well as recruitment and radicalization efforts. The exact amount of profits generated by these illicit activities in the region is unclear, but it is likely—and at least—in the tens of millions of dollars.

External Actors: Iran and Islamic Extremist Groups. Lebanese Hezbollah has long considered the region a potential attack venue against Israeli and other Western targets, and I remain concerned that the group maintains an operational presence there. Lebanese Hezbollah's partner and sponsor, Iran, has sought closer ties with regional governments, largely to circumvent sanctions and counter U.S. influence. As a state-sponsor of terrorism, Iran's involvement in the Western Hemisphere is a matter for concern. Additionally, members, supporters, and adherents of Islamic extremist groups are present in Latin America. Islamic extremists visit the region to proselytize, recruit, establish business venues to generate funds, and expand their radical networks. Some Muslim communities in the Caribbean and South America are exhibiting increasingly extremist ideology and activities, mostly as a result from ideologues' activities and external influence from the Middle East, Africa, and South Asia. Mr. Chairman, we take all these activities seriously, and we and our partners remain vigilant against an evolution in capability of any group with the intent to attack the United States, our interests, or our allies. I remain concerned, however, that U.S. Southern Command's limited intelligence assets may prevent full awareness of the activities of Iranian and terrorist support networks in the region.

Other External Actors. Mr. Chairman, there has been a great deal of attention on the increased regional influence of so-called "external actors" such as China and Russia. Ultimately, we should remember that engagement is not a zero-sum game. Russia and China's expanding relationships are not *necessarily* at our expense. However, if we want to maintain our partnerships in this hemisphere and maintain even minimal influence, we must *remain engaged* with this hemisphere. Budget cuts are having a direct and detrimental effect on our security cooperation activities, the principal way we engage and promote defense cooperation in the region. The cumulative effect of our reduced engagement is a relative but accelerated decline of trust in our reliability and commitment to the region. Our relationships, our leadership, and our influence in the Western Hemisphere are paying the price.

Russia continues to build on its existing strategic partnerships in Latin America, pursuing an increased regional presence through arm sales, counterdrug cooperation, and bilateral trade agreements. Last year marked a noticeable uptick in Russian power projection and security force personnel in the region. It has been over three decades since we last saw this type of high-profile Russian military presence: a visit by a Russian Navy Interfleet Surface Action Group to Cuba, Nicaragua, and Venezuela, and the deployment of two Russian long-range strategic bombers to Venezuela and Nicaragua as part of a training exercise.

As part of its long-term strategy for the region, China is also expanding relationships in Latin America, especially in the Caribbean. In contrast to the Russians,

Chinese engagement is focused primarily on economics, but it uses all elements of national power to achieve its goals. Major investments include potentially $40 billion to construct an alternative to the Panama Canal in Nicaragua and $3 billion to Costa Rica and Caribbean nations for myriad infrastructure and social development projects. China is the single biggest source of financing to Venezuela and Ecuador, due to China's thirst for natural resources and contracts for Chinese state-owned companies. Chinese companies hold notable investments in at least five major ports and are major vendors of telecommunications services to 18 nations in the region. In the defense realm, Chinese technology companies are partnering with Venezuela, Brazil, and Bolivia to launch imagery and communications satellites, and China is gradually increasing its military outreach, offering educational exchanges with many regional militaries. In 2013, the Chinese Navy conducted a goodwill visit in Brazil, Chile, and Argentina and conducted its first-ever naval exercise with the Argentine Navy.

Mr. Chairman, I am often asked if I view engagement by these "external actors" as a direct threat to the United States. Generally speaking, I see potential for greater partnership with China in areas such as humanitarian assistance and disaster response. However, I would like to see the Chinese place greater emphasis on respecting human rights—like we do—as part of their overall engagement efforts in the region. The U.S. government continues to encourage China to address shared security challenges in a positive way, such as taking concrete steps to address the massive illicit trafficking of counterfeit pharmaceuticals and precursor chemicals used for methamphetamine and heroin production in Central America and Mexico. While Russian counterdrug cooperation could potentially contribute to regional security, the sudden increase in its military outreach merits closer attention, as Russia's motives are unclear. Given its history, the region is sensitive to any appearance of increased militarization, which is why it is important that Russia and China promote their defense cooperation in a responsible, transparent manner that helps maintain hemispheric stability and hard-won democratic gains.

Command Priorities

Mr. Chairman, the U.S. military plays an integral role in a whole-of-government approach to address many of these regional security issues. To advance the President's vision and the Department of Defense's policy for the Americas in a resource-constrained environment, U.S. Southern Command focuses our efforts on four priorities. We can accomplish quite a lot with relatively modest investment, but continued budget limitations imperil our ability to build on this progress.

Priority: Detention Operations. Mr. Chairman, I want to speak for a moment about the most important people at Guantanamo: the outstanding men and women that are part of the Joint Task Force at Guantanamo Bay. First, I want to make clear—we who wear the uniform are responsible for one thing at Joint Task Force Guantanamo: detention operations, a mission of enormous complexity and sensitivity. We do not make policy; we follow the orders of the President and Secretary of Defense with the utmost professionalism and integrity.

I have never been prouder of any troops under my command than I am of the young military professionals who stand duty day and night at Guantanamo, serving under a microscope of public scrutiny in one of the toughest and most unforgiving military missions on the planet. These young men and women are charged with caring for detainees that can often be defiant and violent. Our guard and medical forces endure constant insults, taunts, physical assaults, and splashing of bodily fluids by detainees intent on eliciting a reaction.

And in response, each and every military member at Guantanamo exhibits professionalism, patience, and restraint. This is the story that never gets written: that our service members treat every detainee—even the most disruptive and violent among them—with respect, humanity, and dignity, in accordance with all applicable international and U.S. law. Our troops take very seriously their responsibility to provide for the detainees' safe and humane care. In my opinion, *this* story is worth telling, because our country needs to understand that the young Americans sent by the President and the Congress to do this mission are exceptional; they live and work by an unbreakable code of honor and courage and are among the best one percent of their generation.

Mr. Chairman, as you are aware, I am responsible not just for the welfare of my troops, but also for the welfare of every detainee under my care at Joint Task Force Guantanamo. Over the past year, we implemented improvements to enhance the well-being of the detainees. To adequately address the complex medical issues of the aging detainee population, we expanded and emphasized detailed reporting within our comprehensive system to monitor the health, nutrition, and wellness of every detainee. Last year, some detainees went on self-proclaimed "hunger strikes," although many of these detainees continued to consume meals—maintaining or even gaining weight throughout the "strike"—and were at no medical risk. As you know, we have transitioned away from publicly releasing tallies of such hunger strike claims, which in our experience had served to encourage detainee non-compliance and had left the public with a very distorted picture of the overall health of the detainee population.

We continue to support ongoing military commissions, habeas corpus proceedings, periodic review boards, and visits by Congressional and foreign government delegations and non-governmental organizations like the International Committee of the Red Cross. We have taken steps to reduce costs and expenses wherever possible, while continuing to maintain the level of humane care that makes Joint Task Force Guantanamo a model for detention operations worldwide. We reduced the cost of the program supporting the detainee library by 45 percent, and reduced contract requirements and expenses in the Intelligence and Security Program, saving an estimated $6.1 million per year. We also worked with the International Committee of the Red Cross to provide expanded Skype capability to improve detainees' regular communication with family members, at no cost to U.S. taxpayers.

Concerns. Although detention operations have not been adversely affected by budget cuts, I remain concerned by two issues at Guantanamo: advanced medical care and deteriorating infrastructure. Although Naval Station Guantanamo and detainee hospitals are capable of providing adequate care for most detainee conditions, we lack certain specialty medical capabilities necessary to treat potentially complex emergencies and various chronic diseases. In the event a detainee is in need of emergency medical treatment that exceeds on-island capacity, I cannot evacuate him to the United States, as I would a service member.

As a former commander once remarked, we have not been doing detention operations at Guantanamo for twelve years, we have been doing them for one year, twelve times. The expeditionary infrastructure put in place was intended to be temporary, and numerous facilities are showing signs of deterioration and require frequent repair. First and most urgently, some facilities are critical to ensuring the safety and welfare of our troops stationed at Joint Task Force Guantanamo and for the continued humane treatment and health of the detainees. For example, the mess hall—a temporary structure built in the 1990s to support mass migration operations—is at significant risk of structural failure and is corroding after eleven years of continuous use, with holes in the roof and structural support beams. This facility must provide food services to all detainees and over 2,000 assigned personnel on a daily basis. As another example, the High Value Detention Facility is increasingly unsustainable due to drainage and foundation issues. Additionally, I am concerned over inadequate housing for our troops. This housing has other long-term requirements even after detention operations at Guantanamo end; it will be utilized by Naval Station Guantanamo to support a full range of

On October 5, 2013, a U.S.-contracted aircraft carrying one U.S. service member, four DOD contractors, and a Panamanian Air National Guardsman crashed in Colombia, killing four crew members, three of whom were U.S. citizens. The crew was monitoring coastal drug trafficking lanes in the Western Caribbean in support of Operation MARTILLO.

Title 10 missions and nationally-directed contingency requirements for disaster response or mass migration. I am working within the Office of the Secretary of Defense to find solutions to these ongoing facility issues.

Priority: Countering Transnational Organized Crime (CTOC). In response to the challenges posed by the spread of transnational organized crime, U.S. Southern

Command is working with our interagency partners to counter the threats posed by criminal networks and illicit trafficking, focusing on those networks that threaten citizen safety in the region and the security of the United States. Mr. Chairman, our contribution to this effort is relatively small but important, and comes with real sacrifice. In 2013, the crash of a counternarcotics flight in Colombia led to the tragic death of Air Force Master Sergeant Martin Gonzales, two other dedicated American contractors, and a Panamanian officer, and the serious injury of the two pilots, highlighting the true human cost of this fight. The individuals who died will be remembered for their service and their commitment to fighting drug trafficking and criminal networks whose products are killing so many of our countrymen and women every year.

Support to CTOC Efforts in Central America. Last year, we redirected our focus to Central American security institutions involved in appropriate defense missions like border and maritime security. This refinement capitalizes on minimal Department of Defense resources, while also being sensitive to perceptions of militarization of the region. We are prioritizing our support to interagency counter-threat finance efforts and expanding our focus on converging threats, including illicit trafficking via commercial shipping containers, which could be exploited to move weapons of mass destruction into the United States. By supporting the targeting of key illicit financial nodes and commercial linkages, we aim to help degrade the capacities of both criminal and terrorist groups.

Now entering its third year, Operation MARTILLO continues to demonstrate commitment by the United States, our partner nations and European allies to counter the spread of transnational criminal organizations and protect citizens in Central America from the violence, harm, and exploitation wrought by criminal networks. However, force allocation cuts by the Services are taking their toll on operational results; in 2013, Operation MARTILLO disrupted 132 metric tons of cocaine, compared with 152 metric tons of cocaine in 2012, due to limited assets.

On a positive note, the operation has led to improved interoperability and increased partner nation contributions. Our partners helped prevent 66 metric tons of cocaine from reaching the United States last year; 50 percent of Joint Interagency Task Force South's successes would not have occurred without the participation of partner nations. Limited and declining Department

Operation MARTILLO FY 13 Disruptions	
Cocaine	132,191 kgs
Marijuana	41,232 lbs
Bulk cash	$3.5 million
Conveyances	107

of Defense assets will influence the next phase of the operation, as Operation MARTILLO's original objectives may no longer be achievable. In the year ahead, we will seek to employ non-traditional solutions, within our current authorities, to partially mitigate detection and monitoring shortfalls. However, lack of assets will continue to constrain the operation's full effectiveness, and has the potential to be perceived as lack of political will on the part of the U.S. government to continue this fight.

Interagency Partnerships. Our CTOC efforts focus on providing support to our law enforcement partners. These partnerships ensure a whole of government approach to both operations and capacity building efforts. To mitigate asset shortfalls, we rely heavily on the U.S. Coast Guard and Customs and Border Protection, which now provide the bulk of the ships and aircraft available to disrupt drugs bound for the United States. The heroic men and women of DEA's Foreign Deployed Advisory and Support Team (FAST) provide critical support to partner nation interdiction operations, and we are fortunate to have nine DEA Special Investigative Units working to improve regional law enforcement capacity. In my view, DEA is a known, essential partner, and their focus on building the investigative and intelligence capacities of vetted law enforcement units complements our own efforts to professionalize regional defense and security forces.

In late 2013, U.S. Southern Command and the Treasury Department created a Counter-Threat Finance Branch, an analytical unit that will map illicit networks, combat the financial underpinnings of national security threats in the region, and support the development of targeted financial measures and U.S. law enforcement actions. As one example, we provided

U.S. Southern Command has 34 representatives from 15 different federal agencies assigned and embedded in our headquarters staff.

analytic support to the Treasury Department's financial sanctions against Los Cachiros in Honduras. We also work with Immigration and Customs Enforcement to aggressively target criminal networks that traffic in special interest aliens and contraband throughout the region. Additionally, U.S. Southern Command and the FBI expanded their analytic partnership to include the FBI's International Operations and Criminal Investigative Divisions. This enhanced partnership helps both agencies further develop partner nation capacity in countering transnational organized crime. We also partnered with the Department of Homeland Security to provide network analysis in support of Operation CITADEL, which targeted the movements of illicit proceeds in Central America. In Colombia, we are working with the Joint Improvised Explosive Device Defeat Organization to assist our Colombian partners in countering the threat of improvised explosive devices (IEDs) used by terrorist groups like the FARC. Finally, we are also coordinating with the Department of State's Bureaus of International Narcotics and Law Enforcement and Western Hemisphere Affairs to explore the possibility of providing logistical support to regional law enforcement operations.

Impact of Budget Cuts—CTOC. Severe budget constraints are significantly degrading our ability defend the southern approaches to the United States. Sequestration merely compounds the ongoing challenge of limited and declining U.S. government maritime and air assets required for detection, monitoring, and "end-game" interdiction missions. Irrespective of sequestration cuts, we face a sharp downtown in availability of large surface assets such as U.S. Navy frigates and U.S. Coast Guard High Endurance Cutters, which face decommissioning or are approaching the end of their expected lifespan. The eighth and final U.S. Coast Guard National Security Cutter, which will be delivered in the next few years, will be a critical asset to U.S. government efforts to protect our southern approaches.

Mr. Chairman, the impact of diminishing asset allocation will continue to impede our mission even if sequestration is reversed; our operational effectiveness is directly proportional to the number

In 2013, Joint Interagency Task Force South was unable to take action on 74% of actionable illicit trafficking events due to lack of assets.

of assets we can put against detection, monitoring, and interdiction operations. When better resourced several years ago, we were able to disrupt a significant amount—more than 240 metric tons—of cocaine heading towards the United States. Last year, 20 more metric tons of cocaine reached the United States due to reduced asset availability, a number that will increase inversely as the availability of U.S. government assets decreases.

Other Issues. Additionally, I remain concerned over the planned construction of wind farm sites in North Carolina that will interfere with our Relocatable Over-The-Horizon Radar (ROTHR) radar system in Virginia. I am also concerned over wind projects in Texas that will impact ROTHR systems in that state. These wind farms could and likely will adversely impact our ROTHR systems, the only persistent wide-area surveillance radars capable of tracking illicit aircraft in Latin America and the Caribbean. We are working within the Department of Defense and with developers and stakeholders to develop potential mitigation solutions, but I have little confidence we will succeed.

Priority: Building Partner Capacity. Having strong partners is the cornerstone of U.S. Southern Command's engagement strategy and is essential for our national

security. Capable and effective partners respect human rights, share in the costs and responsibilities of ensuring regional security, and help us detect, deter, and interdict threats *before* they reach the U.S. homeland. Our persistent human rights engagement also helps encourage defense cooperation, trust, and confidence, which cannot be surged when a crisis hits, and cannot be achieved through episodic deployments or chance contacts. Trust must be built, nurtured, and sustained through regular contact.

Engagement with Colombia. Our partner Colombia has paid the ultimate price in terms of their blood and national treasure to bring the FARC—who have been serial human rights violators

According to a Colombian NGO, between 2001 and 2009, nearly 750,000 women were victims of sexual violence, rape, and enslavement at the hands of illegally armed groups like the FARC.

for decades—to the negotiating table. The Colombians have fought heroically for a peaceful, democratic Colombia, which will be a powerful symbol of hope and prosperity, but it is far too soon to declare victory. Mr. Chairman, it is absolutely imperative we remain engaged as one of our strongest allies works to consolidate its hard-won success. To that end, U.S. Southern Command is providing advice and assistance to the Colombian military's transformation efforts, as it works to improve interoperability and transition to an appropriate role in post-conflict Colombia. With Colombia increasingly taking on the role of security exporter, we are facilitating the deployment of Colombian-led training teams and subject matter experts and attendance of Central American personnel to law enforcement and military academies in Colombia as part of the U.S.-Colombia Action Plan on Regional Security Cooperation. This is a clear example of a sizeable return on our relatively modest investment and sustained engagement.

Engagement in South America. In Peru, U.S. Southern Command and the DEA are working together to support Peru's ongoing efforts against the Shining Path, which are beginning to yield significant operational successes. An investment of 6 U.S. personnel, who trained

In 2013, U.S. Southern Command facilitated the delivery of life-saving medicine to 140 patients in Brazil following a tragic nightclub fire.

combat medical instructors from Peru and El Salvador, resulted in the training of over 2,000 members of the Peruvian and Salvadoran military, including Salvadoran soldiers destined for stability operations in Afghanistan, Lebanon, and Haiti. We are working with Chile on capacity-building efforts in Central America and exploring possible future engagements in the Pacific. In Brazil, broader bilateral challenges have affected our defense relations. Our military-to-military cooperation at the operational and tactical levels, however, remains strong, and we are committed to supporting the United States' growing global partnership with Brazil. We continue to engage with Brazilian security forces in the run-up to the 2014 World Cup and 2016 Olympics. Brazil participated in several of our multinational exercises last year, including playing a leading role in PANAMAX, which focuses on the defense of the Panama Canal.

Engagement in Central America. In 2013, U.S. Southern Command provided critical infrastructure and operational support to the new Guatemalan Interagency Task Force, which has contributed to significant disruption of illicit trafficking along the Guatemalan-Mexican border and is now viewed by the Government of Guatemala as a model for future units. In collaboration with U.S. Northern Command, we are planning initiatives in Guatemala and Belize to support Mexico's new southern border strategy. I recently visited Guatemala and was struck by the government's strong commitment to work with human rights groups and strengthen its democratic institutions, while also doing its part to stem the massive flow of illicit trafficking heading to our country. Unfortunately, current legislative restrictions on provisions such as Foreign Military Financing and International Military Education and Training, found in the FY14 Consolidated Appropriations Act, limit the United States' ability to fully engage with the Guatemalan military and security forces. In another example of successful interagency partnerships, Joint Task Force Bravo supported the Belizean Defense Force and DEA in the eradication of 100,446 marijuana plants and the seizure of 330 pounds of marijuana.

Along Panama's Pacific Coast, we constructed three key maritime facilities and are providing counternarcotics training to Panamanian coast guard and maritime security forces. Mr. Chairman, I applaud the Government of Panama in their handling of last year's smuggling incident involving Cuban military equipment aboard a North Korean vessel. We are fortunate to have partners like Panama that are committed to ensuring international security. Finally, I am particularly proud of our support to the

Since 2003, the El Salvador Armed Forces have contributed 11 rotations in support Operation Iraqi Freedom and three rotations in support of Operation Enduring Freedom in Afghanistan.

third deployment of members of the El Salvador Armed Forces to Afghanistan. Augmented by the New Hampshire National Guard, the Salvadoran unit returned this past December from serving as a Police Advisory Team that provided training to Afghan security forces. Like Panama, El Salvador is just one example of the outstanding partners we have in this part of the world—partners that are doing their part to ensure peace and security within and beyond their borders.

Engagement in the Caribbean. Throughout Central America and the Caribbean, U.S. Southern Command has constructed or improved partner nation naval and coast guard operating bases and facilities and delivered more than $3 million in counternarcotics training and non-lethal equipment, including a total of 42 high-speed interceptor boats provided since 2008 that have supported Joint Inter-Agency Task Force (JIATF) South interdiction operations. In support of the Caribbean Basin Security Initiative (CBSI), we are working to improve maritime patrol and intercept capabilities of our Caribbean partners. Through CBSI, a maritime Technical Assistance Field Team— comprised of joint Coast Guard and Department of Defense personnel—provides hands-on technical assistance, in-country mentoring, and training to 13 CBSI partner nations, with the goal of helping these countries develop accountable and sustainable engineering, maintenance, and logistics and procurement systems. The TAFT program is a collaborative interagency effort funded by the U.S. Department of State, using Foreign

Military Financing and INCLE funding. In Haiti, the government is committed to improving its disaster response capabilities. Haiti continues to make gradual social and economic progress after 2010's devastating earthquake, and the Government of Haiti is committed to improving its disaster response capabilities. Led by Brazil and comprised of a multinational force that includes personnel from Uruguay, Chile, and Guatemala, the United Nations Stabilization Mission in Haiti (MINUSTAH) has played a critical role in Haiti's efforts to rebuild, working with the Haitian National Police to ensure security. As MINUSTAH draws down, I see a continued need for international engagement in Haiti to guarantee lasting stability.

Cooperation on Counterterrorism. We also work with the interagency, U.S. Embassy Country Teams, and our partner nations to counter the encroachment of both Sunni and Shi'a Islamic extremism, recruitment, and radicalization efforts that support terrorism activities. We conduct multiple engagement efforts—including Joint Combined Exchange Training, subject matter expert and intelligence exchanges, counterterrorism-focused exercises, and key leader engagements—here in the United States and in countries throughout the region. Sustained engagement helps build relationships, an essential tool in the fight against terrorism. Through intelligence and counterterrorism cooperation, our partners are better able to mitigate terrorist threats before they can cause mass destruction, destabilize a country, or reach the U.S. homeland.

Human Rights and Defense Professionalization. Everything we do at U.S. Southern Command begins and ends with human rights. Mr. Chairman, a lot of people talk about human rights, but the U.S. military *does* human rights. We live it. We teach it. We enforce it. U.S. Southern Command's Human Rights Initiative continued to break new ground in 2013, promoting dialogue and cooperation between regional military forces and human rights groups and strengthening institutional capacity in Guatemala and Honduras. Since its inception, our Human Rights Initiative has helped promote reform throughout the region, and the results speak for themselves. Military forces serving democratic governments in the region understand, and take seriously, their responsibility to respect and protect human rights. Ten partner nations have formally committed to implementing the Human Rights Initiative, building an institutional culture of respect for human rights within their militaries.

U.S. Southern Command also promotes human rights through law of armed conflict programs led by the Defense Institute of Legal Studies and through academic institutions like the Perry Center for Hemispheric Defense Studies, the Western Hemisphere Institute for

In 2013, 1,417 students from the region participated in the International Military Education Training (IMET) program, an invaluable investment in future defense leaders.

Security Cooperation, and the Inter-American Air Forces Academy. Additionally, the entire premise of the International Military Education and Training (IMET) program promotes an environment conducive to students learning and sharing U.S. values and democracy, with human rights portions embedded in nearly every course. Mr. Chairman, IMET is one of our most valuable engagement tools; professional military education improves how our partners work with us in a joint, interoperable world. Participants not only better understand our culture; they share our perspective, and want to work with us to advance U.S. and regional interests.

Cyber Security and Information Operations. In the region, U.S. Southern Command works to ensure the continued security of Department of Defense networks and communication infrastructure. We are also slowly making progress in strengthening regional cyber defense and information operations capabilities. In 2013, U.S. Southern Command, working with the Perry Center, brought together strategy and policy officers from the region to share information on current cyber security threats. Colombia, Chile, and Brazil have each expressed interest in sharing "lessons learned" on building effective cyber security institutions. Through Operation SOUTHERN VOICE, 50 information operation practitioners from 11 Western Hemisphere countries shared capabilities and best practices. In the year ahead, we are partnering with Colombia to build information-related capabilities in Guatemala and Panama, and with U.S. Northern Command to do the same in Mexico.

Multinational Exercises and Humanitarian Assistance. U.S. Southern Command's multinational exercise and humanitarian and civic assistance programs encourage collective action and demonstrate our values and commitment to the region. Last year's UNITAS and TRADEWINDS exercises helped improve interoperability among our hemisphere's maritime forces. During our annual humanitarian and civic

In 2013, we executed 140 minimal cost projects and worked with local populations and non-governmental organizations (NGOs) to construct and supply schools, community shelters, clinics, and hospitals.

assistance exercises NEW HORIZONS and BEYOND THE HORIZONS, U.S. forces improved their readiness and provided medical care to 34,677 patients in El Salvador, Panama, and Belize. These humanitarian missions are one of the most effective tools in our national security toolkit, and one that I believe warrants greater employment. In any given year, we are able to send around 700 medical professionals to the region; Cuba, in contrast, sends around 30,000, mostly to Venezuela. In 2013, our collaboration with the private sector and non-governmental organizations resulted in contributions of $4.3 million in gifts-in-kind and services to our humanitarian activities. Mr. Chairman, I cannot overstate the importance of these types of activities by the U.S. military, especially in terms of influence and access. As Secretary Hagel noted, our humanitarian engagement offers the next generation of global citizens direct experience with the positive impact of American values and ideals.

Perceptions of "Militarization." Mr. Chairman, I want to close this section by responding to the perception by some that our engagement is "militarizing" the region. In my view, these concerns reflect a misunderstanding of the actual role the U.S. military plays in this part of the world. As an example, our Special Operations Forces are among the most qualified, culturally sensitive, and linguistically capable trainers in the U.S. military, and above all, they excel at building trust and forging personal relationships that are essential to supporting our national interests. Whether it's a small team at the tactical level or an official engagement at my level, all our efforts are focused on *professionalizing* military and security forces, to help our partners become more accountable to civilian authority, more capable, and to above all respect the human rights of the citizens they are charged to protect. Our efforts are part of a whole-of-government approach—involving DEA, Department of Justice, Department of Homeland Security, Department of State, and many others—to strengthen governance and foster accountable, transparent, and effective institutions throughout the Western Hemisphere.

Mr. Chairman, engagement by the U.S. military can make a real and lasting difference, especially in terms of promoting respect for human rights. Ultimately, if we want regional militaries to honor, respect, and accept civilian control and demonstrate an institutional culture of respect for human rights, that message must come from a military that lives by that code. For the U.S. military, our own training begins and ends with human rights; it is at the center of everything we do and an integral part of every interaction with partner nations. I regularly meet with human rights groups in Washington and throughout the region, and human rights is a major theme in every engagement with my counterparts in regional militaries.

Throughout the world, the U.S. military has a unique network of alliances and partnerships, and our regional approach can provide a framework for engagement by the broader U.S. interagency. Thanks in part to our efforts, Colombia is now a beacon of hope and stability with one of the most highly professionalized militaries in the region; Central America is now the focus for numerous interagency initiatives; the Caribbean now routinely shares information in support of international counterdrug operations; and perhaps most importantly, today the hemisphere is characterized by militaries under civilian control that recognize their fundamental responsibility to respect human rights. In my mind, there is no more valuable return on engagement than that.

Impact of Budget Cuts—BPC. In FY 13, we began seeing the initial effects of sequestration, which resulted in drastic force allocation cuts by all the Services. In turn, reduced availability of forces adversely impacted our execution of plans and engagement activities. Severe budget constraints are affecting our established military-to-military relationships that took decades to establish, limiting our ability to build on the progress I just described. Mr. Chairman, let me be frank: reduced engagement risks the deterioration of U.S. leadership and influence in Central America, South America, and the Caribbean.

In FY 13, budget uncertainty caused the cancellation of four major exercises, including FUERZAS COMANDO—one of only two exercises focused on counterterrorism—and 225 engagement activities that are critical to building capable and effective defense and security forces in the region. The Navy's cancelled deployment of CONTINUING PROMISE was felt throughout the region; it is our single most impactful humanitarian mission, demonstrating U.S. values and creating goodwill and positive views towards our country. We rely heavily on the National Guard's State Partnership Program to conduct our activities, and the cancellation of 69 events was detrimental to our efforts to maintain long-term security relationships. Reductions in force allocation also created significant gaps in persistent Civil Affairs coverage. The cancellation of Civil Affairs deployments has created a loss of credibility with our partner nations and our partners in U.S. Embassies in the region, who have questioned U.S. Southern Command's ability to fulfill our commitments. Finally, the Perry Center, which helps build capacity at the ministerial level, is facing a severe 50 percent cut in funding over the several upcoming fiscal years.

Priority: Planning for Contingencies. Lastly, planning and preparing for possible contingencies is one of U.S. Southern Command's core missions. Every year, we regularly exercise our rapid response capabilities in a variety of scenarios, including responding to a natural disaster, mass migration event, an attack on the Panama Canal, or evacuating American citizens. In 2013, we conducted our INTEGRATED ADVANCE exercise, which focuses on improving coordination with interagency partners in response to a mass migration event in the Caribbean. On this issue, we are fortunate to have an excellent exercise, operational, and planning relationship with Homeland Security Task

Force Southeast, and together we work to defend the southern approaches to the United States. That mission, however, continues to be significantly impacted by force allocation cuts.

Impact of Budget Cuts—Contingency Response. Mr. Chairman, our ability to respond to regional contingencies such as a mass migration event or natural disaster was impaired in 2013, a trend that could continue in 2014. U.S. Southern Command has minimal assigned and allocated forces, and we rely on the Services—especially the Navy—to "surge" forces and assets when a crisis hits. As the Services absorb large reductions to their budgets, this will affect U.S. Southern Command's ability to immediately respond to crises and disasters, which could lead to preventable human suffering and loss-of-life. As I mentioned earlier, I am deeply concerned by the uptick in Haitian migration in the Mona Passage and the continued scarcity of U.S. government assets in the Caribbean. As currently resourced, U.S. Southern Command faces considerable challenges to rapidly support a mass migration response.

Our People

Headquarters Budget. Mr. Chairman, as you can see, we can accomplish a lot with a relatively small portion of the Department of Defense budget. Last year, the forced furloughs of 572 civilian employees had a significant impact on our ability to conduct our missions. Fortunately, the temporary budget reprieve should spare our workforce the pain of furloughs in FY 14 and FY 15, but continued budget uncertainty will likely lead to an inevitable "talent drain" as our best and brightest civilian employees seek more stable employment opportunities. Although we appreciate the near-term budget solution, the long-term challenge of sequestration has not been resolved. It has merely been deferred.

Partial Mitigation to Budget Cuts. Per guidance from the Office of the Secretary of Defense, U.S. Southern Command must strive for a goal of 20 percent reductions in our headquarters budget and military and civilian personnel by FY 2019. Combined with the potential of continued sequestration, resource cuts require a fundamental re-look at what U.S. Southern Command will and will not be able to do with limited resources. Due to ongoing resource constraints, I have directed a transformation effort at our headquarters to look holistically at our strategy and resources. Limited defense dollars

To ensure our workforce has mission-critical capabilities, our Joint Training Program offered training opportunities to 85 military and civilian joint staff officers, and also delivered cultural training to enhance our interactions in the region.

must be applied wisely, and we are seeking to preserve our core military missions and functions. As we work through this process, we will continue to emphasize our partnerships with the interagency, NGOs, and private sector to help mitigate ongoing fiscal challenges. U.S. Southern Command has proven success in this area, averaging $16 million in return on investment annually from this collaboration, all of it directly impacting our missions.

Support Services. U.S. Southern Command's most important resource is its Soldiers, Sailors, Airmen, Marines, Coast Guardsman, and civilian employees. The safety and security of our people is of utmost importance, and I am concerned by the severe funding cuts to the security force that guards our headquarters. Additionally, my assigned service members, especially junior enlisted personnel, continue to face significant financial hardships trying to make ends meet under the current Cost of Living

Allowance—a mere $28 for an E3 and just $33 for an E9—in Miami, one of the most expensive cities in the world, especially when it comes to car and home insurance rates.[12] Compounding this concern is the uncertainty over military compensation and reductions in retirement benefits.

Our family support services also face significant funding strains, forcing us to breach sacred promises to our Armed Forces families. We take suicide prevention very seriously at our headquarters, and last year we delivered four separate programs aimed at preventing suicides and raising awareness. However, the Army was forced to decrement support services at nearly every installation and facility, including U.S. Army Garrison Miami. As a result, our Substance Abuse and Suicide Prevention Programs have lost the Clinical/Treatment Program and will lose both the Prevention Program Coordinator and the Suicide Program Manager/Employee Assistance Coordinator by 2015.

Conclusion

Mr. Chairman, in closing I would like to offer a personal observation from my first year in command. This region does not ask for much. Most nations in this part of the world *want* our partnership, our friendship, and our support. They *want* to work with us, because they recognize that we share many of the same values and interests, many of the same challenges and concerns. Some of my counterparts perceive that the United States is disengaging from the region and from the world in general. We should

---

[12] UBS. Pricings and Earnings Report, Edition 2012. Geneva: September, 2012; Center for Housing Policy. Losing Ground: The Struggle for Middle Income Households to Afford the Risings Costs of Housing and Transportation. October 2012. According to apartment market research firm AXOIMetrics, the average effective rent (which includes concessions) in Miami is $1,269 per month, compared to the U.S. as a whole at $964. According to the Joint Center for Housing Studies at Harvard University, the Miami rental market has the greatest share of severely cost-burdened renters (i.e. renters who pay more than half their income to rent) in the country.

remember that our friends and allies are not the only ones watching our actions closely. Reduced engagement could itself become a national security problem, with long-term, detrimental effects on U.S. leadership, access, and interests in a part of the world where our engagement has made a real and lasting difference. And in the meantime, drug traffickers, criminal networks, and other actors, unburdened by budget cuts, cancelled activities, and employee furloughs, will have the opportunity to exploit the partnership vacuum left by reduced U.S. military engagement. Thank you.

- **Security Cooperation:** ARSOUTH conducted 166 security cooperation events in 19 countries in U.S. Southern Command's area of responsibility. These events represent 166 instances of engagement and building partner nation capabilities with the other militaries in the region. **Building Partner Nation Capacity to Counter Terrorism:** ARSOUTH conducted 26 Subject Matter Expert Exchanges in ten countries that included over 800 host nation soldiers. The engagements included: Medical, Mountain Operations, Search and Rescue, Logistics, Force Protection, Communications and Personal Security Detail.

- **Countering Transnational Organized Crime (CTOC):** ARSOUTH conducted training with the newly organized Guatemalan Interagency Task Force (IATF). The IATF consists of 242 personnel from the Army, Police, Customs, and Attorney General's Office. Training consisted of instruction focused on driving tactical vehicles, basic tactics, weapons qualification on all assigned systems, Harris Radio procedures, logistics, combat lifesaving, advanced maneuver, combat medic, and crowd control. The IATF is currently conducting border security operations on the Guatemala/Mexico border.

- **Civil Military Relations:** Civil Military Relations Professional Development Exchanges provide a forum for bilateral executive-level information exchanges. Participants include Partner Nation Civil Affairs Officers and Government Officials, U.S. Military and government officials, National Guard State Partnership Program representatives, and Non-Governmental and Intergovernmental Organizations. ARSOUTH conducted Civil Military Relations Professional Development Exchanges in Belize, El Salvador, Guatemala, and Honduras, improving the ability of these countries to conduct inter-organizational coordination during humanitarian assistance and disaster relief operations.

- **Personnel Recovery Operations:** ARSOUTH conducted seven engagements with six countries, focused on increasing partner nation capabilities and capacity to conduct search and rescue operations. This focus was a direct result of lessons learned during the Haiti earthquake. Due to budget uncertainty, ARSOUTH has significantly reduced engagement planning in FY 14 and FY 15.

- **Intelligence Security Cooperation:** The ARSOUTH Intelligence Team conducted 18 major Intelligence Security Cooperation engagement activities enabling military intelligence capacity building in support of countering transnational threats in the following countries: Brazil, Colombia, El Salvador, Guatemala, Honduras, Panama and Peru.

- **Logistics Security Cooperation:** The ARSOUTH Logistics Team conducted 25 Security Cooperation engagements, which enabled military logistics capacity building in support of CTOC, Staff Talk Agreements, and Building Partner Nation Capacity in 10 countries.

- **Latin American Cooperation:** ARSOUTH Latin American Cooperation Funds (LACF) supported 46 engagements/activities in eight countries in support of ARSOUTH Security Cooperation objectives. LACF support includes: Army-to-

Army Staff Talks with key countries, Foreign Liaison Officers assigned to ARSOUTH, Conference of American Armies, professional development exchanges on multiple topics, Army commander and distinguished visitor program, and Joint/Combined/Multinational Exercises and Operations.

- **Humanitarian Assistance Program (HAP):** HAP conducts activities to build partner nation capacity in providing essential services to its civilian population including, responding to disaster and other crises; reinforcing security; and sustaining stability in a host nation or region. ARSOUTH, the HAP construction program manager, completed ten projects in Belize, Panama and Peru, and initiated planning for 19 new construction projects in Belize, Guatemala, Honduras, Panama, and Peru.

- **Global Peace Operations Initiative (GPOI):** GPOI is a U.S. government-funded security assistance program to enhance international capacity to effectively conduct United Nations and regional peace support operations. ARSOUTH, the GPOI construction program manager, completed four GPOI projects in Guatemala, Paraguay, and Peru, and initiated planning for 4 new construction projects in El Salvador and Guatemala.

- **Staff Talks:** ARSOUTH, representing the Army Chief of Staff, conducted four Steering Committee Meetings and four Executive Session Staff Talks with the Armies of Brazil, Chile, Colombia, and El Salvador, and one Working Group with Peru resulting in strengthened key leader relationships and more than 130 Agreed-to-Actions planned through 2018, supporting bilateral and regional goals and interests.

- **INTEGRATED ADVANCE 2013:** INTEGRATED ADVANCE 2013, a joint operational exercise, focused on conducting migrant operations in the Caribbean Sea, marked the first large scale deployment of ARSOUTH personnel and capabilities since Operation Unified Response in Haiti in 2010. Over 300 U.S. Army personnel, 100 sister service personnel, and almost 100 personnel from other governmental agencies came together in a whole-of-government response. INTEGRATED ADVANCE 2013 exercised ARSOUTH's commitment to form the core of a US Southern Command Joint Task Force, rapidly integrate other joint and interagency forces, and conduct mission command of joint operations.

- **PANAMAX 2013:** PANAMAX is a joint and combined operational exercise focused on the defense of the Panama Canal by a multi-national joint task force. USSOUTHCOM significantly de-scoped PANAMAX 2013 resulting in a small table-top exercise focused on conducting mission planning in a time-constrained environment. ARSOUTH provided mentorship to the Brazilian led Combined Forces Land Component Command, which included 38 participants from nine countries. This exercise coincided with the first major deployment of an ARSOUTH team to Panama to participate in a Government of Panama national exercise (PANAMAX – Alpha). This team of 40 U.S. personnel worked with the Government of Panama coordinating U.S. forces assistance during a simulated national disaster event to significantly increase cooperation and trust between the Governments of Panama and the United States.

- **BEYOND THE HORIZON 2013:** BEYOND THE HORIZON is a Chairman of the Joint Chiefs of Staff, US Southern Command-sponsored Joint, Interagency, and Combined Field Training Exercise. The exercise provides and incorporates Humanitarian and Civic Assistance construction projects, Medical Readiness

Exercises, and other infrastructure projects. ARSOUTH was the executive planning agent for these exercises conducted in El Salvador and Panama, which involved the deployment of approximately 2700 U.S. service members into two supported countries. BEYOND THE HORIZON 2013 resulted in the completion of 11 engineer projects including schools and clinics, 4 Medical Readiness Exercises, one Dental Readiness Exercise and one Specialty Medical Readiness Exercise that provided care to approximately 23,641 patients and approximately 6,634 animals for veterinary support. The exercises were supported by over 200 El Salvadoran and Panamanian military and interagency personnel working side-by-side with U.S. personnel.

- **Conference of the American Armies (CAA):** The Conference of the American Armies (25 countries and two International Military Organizations) contributes to peacekeeping operations and disaster relief operations through the creation and use of mechanisms and procedures that improve the collective capacities and interoperability of its members. This year, ARSOUTH represented the Army Chief of Staff at the Emerging Threats Conference in Colombia, Disaster Relief exercise in Mexico, Extraordinary Commander's Conference in Mexico, Civil-Military Cooperation Exercise in Canada, Environmental Conference in Brazil, IED Ad-Hoc meeting in Colombia, Procedures Training & Education conference in Uruguay, Communications exercise via CAA Webpage, Army commanders VTC and the Preparatory Commanders Conference in Mexico.

- **Reintegration:** ARSOUTH, as supported Commander for Personnel Recovery Phase III (Reintegration operations), executed a Reintegration Operation following the crash of an operational theater aircraft. The aircraft was operating over Colombia in support of Operation MARTILLO. Following the successful recovery of the survivors by the Colombian Army, ARSOUTH coordinated transfer and movement of the survivors to Brooke Army Medical Center, San Antonio, Texas where all aspects of the reintegration were completed.

- **Continuous Operational Intelligence Support:** The ARSOUTH Intelligence Team provided continuous intelligence reach-back support and direct support forward to Joint Task Force Bravo, Joint Interagency Task Force South, Joint Task Force Guantanamo Bay, the U.S. Interagency, and partner nations in Central and South America in support of numerous named operations. Throughout the year, persistent forward intelligence, surveillance and reconnaissance (ISR) support was maintained in Colombia, Guatemala, and Honduras. U.S. Army Force Protection Detachments also maintained permanent presence in nine countries.

U.S. Naval Forces Southern Command (COMUSNAVSO)
Headquarters: Mayport, Florida

- **Operation MARTILLO:** Six frigates, High Speed Vessel (HSV) SWIFT, four fixed-wing Maritime Patrol aircraft and two Scientific Development Squadron ONE detachments deployed to support Operation MARTILLO, conducting Countering

Transnational Organized Crime (C-TOC) Operations under the direction of Joint Interagency Task Force South.

- **Southern Partnership Station 2013:** Southern Partnership Station (SPS) is a series of Navy/Marine Corps engagements focused on Theater Security Cooperation, specifically Building Partner Capacity, through subject matter expert exchanges with partner nation militaries and civilian security forces. SPS engagements include Community Relations Projects that focus on our partnerships, shared interests, and shared values. SPS Deployments included:
  - ➤ **HSV 2013:** HSV SWIFT deployed to the U.S. Southern Command (USSOUTHCOM) area of responsibility (AOR) February to May 2013 to conduct Building Partner Capacity engagements in Belize, Guatemala, and Honduras, and to participate in Operation MARTILLO.
  - ➤ **Oceanographic 2013:** Survey Ship USNS PATHFINDER conducted bilateral hydrographic surveys with Chile in the Eastern Pacific and with Panama in the Caribbean and Eastern Pacific.
- **PANAMAX 2013:** Commander USNAVSO served as the Commander of Multi-National Forces South, leading a coalition of 19 partner nations in the 11th annual exercise designed to execute stability operations under the support of UN Security Council Resolutions, provide interoperability training for participating multinational staffs, and build partner nation capacity to plan and execute complex multinational operations. PANAMAX 13 was executed as a table-top exercise, and focused on multinational crisis action planning.
- **UNITAS 2013:** Commander USNAVSO planned and executed the 54th iteration of multinational maritime exercise UNITAS, which included 16 partner nations, 17 ships, one submarine, and 12 helicopters and aircraft. Conducted every year since 1960, UNITAS is the longest-running international military training exercise in the world. Colombia employed maritime forces in cooperative maritime security operations in order to maintain access, enhance interoperability, and build enduring partnerships that foster regional security in the USSOUTHCOM AOR.
- **INTEGRATED ADVANCE 2013:** USNAVSO participated in Exercise INTEGRATED ADVANCE 2013, which examined a whole-of-government response to a Caribbean Mass Migration crisis. USNAVSO provided the deputy commander for Joint Task Force Migrant Operations, while also designating Destroyer Squadron FOUR ZERO as the Joint Force Maritime Component Commander and standing up a Maritime Coordination and Control Element within the Joint Task Force construct. The highly successful exercise focused on strengthening interoperability and cooperation between DOD and Interagency organizations.
- **Continuing Promise 2013:** In lieu of CONTINUING PROMISE 2013, a team of Navy medical providers conducted medical exchanges with Peru and Honduras, working side-by-side with partner nation medical professionals to generate a baseline for future CONTINUING PROMISE Missions.
- **Navy Seabees:** 85 Seabees deployed to Naval Station Guantanamo Bay to support construction/refurbishment projects throughout the USSOUTHCOM AOR. From this detachment, Seabee details deployed in support of HSV SPS 2013 and Operation MARTILLO while also completing projects in support of Naval Station Guantanamo Bay and the Joint Task Force Guantanamo Bay Commander. Additionally, Seabees

supported Naval Station Guantanamo Bay with Public Works Officer discretionary projects and clean-up/relief projects following Hurricane Sandy. Following the cancelation of Continuing Promise 2013, the Seabees still supported a Subject Matter Expert Exchange with Peruvian Engineers.

12th Air Force (Air Forces Southern)
Headquarters: Tucson, Arizona

- **Security Cooperation:** Air Forces Southern (AFSOUTH) conducted 19 security cooperation events in eight countries in U.S. Southern Command's area of responsibility. Engagements focused on improving partner nation communications, maintenance, intelligence, air patrol operations, space capabilities, close air support, public affairs, and flight medicine capabilities.
- **Sovereign Skies Expansion Program:** AFSOUTH used successful lessons learned from the Dominican Republic and Colombia programs to strengthen air force capabilities in El Salvador, Guatemala, and Honduras. Training included helicopter maintenance; ISR; logistics; command and control; and night operations.
- **571 Mobility Support Advisory Squadron (MSAS):** MSAS completed six deployments of air adviser teams to Peru, Guatemala, Uruguay, Honduras, and two to Colombia, while training 313 partner nation military members. MSAS delivers some of the Air Force's highest return on investment in partner nation capabilities, resulting in trainee compliance with NATO, International Civil Aviation Organization and FAA standards, and enabling participation in coalition exercises and regional security initiatives. MSAS's achievements have been praised by multiple partner nation air chiefs.
- **NEW HORIZONS 2013 (Belize):** AFSOUTH trained 471 US Airmen, Soldiers, and Marine personnel in joint/combined/interagency environments, in addition to 10 Canadian Medical Personnel, 40 Belize Defense Force (BDF) Engineers, over 100 BDF Security Personnel, and five Project Hope volunteer participants. Personnel built 4 classroom buildings and hurricane shelters with 17,000 square feet for teachers and 430 students; constructed 3 playgrounds; restored 3 schools and one shelter, increasing hurricane shelter capacity by 900; and treated over 18,000 patients through eight medical operations. Subject Matter Expert Exchanges covered maternal & child health, public health and biomedical equipment topics.
- **ISR Missions:** AFSOUTH provided command and control for ISR missions in support of USSOUTHCOM priorities. Over 900 missions and 4,600 flight hours resulted in over 28,000 images, 2,000 signals intelligence reports and nearly 17,000 minutes of video resulting in the largest drug seizure in Belize history – $12.5 million worth of marijuana. AFSOUTH also deployed a ground-based radar to Honduras for 90 days supporting Operation MARTILLO, facilitating the interdiction of 1.4 metric tons of cocaine and seven aircraft.
- **Airlift Missions:** AFSOUTH executed 95 theater airlift missions moving more than 5,000 passengers and 200 tons of cargo throughout USSOUTHCOM's area of responsibility.

- **Medical Deployments:** AFSOUTH International Health Specialists participated in global health Subject Matter Expert Exchange engagements to address Flight Medicine topics relevant to our partner nations. USAF flight medicine physicians met with Colombian counterparts to develop aerospace physiology programs addressing safety, human factors and hypobaric chambers, and focusing on aeromedical standards and aeromedical evacuation/patient movement/critical care air transport teams.

-

Marine Corps Forces South (MARFORSOUTH)
Headquarters: Doral, Florida

- **Building Partner Capacity:** MARFORSOUTH employed multiple assets to support partner nation and interagency efforts to counter regional threats throughout South and Central America.
  - ➢ In Central America, MARFORSOUTH developed partner nation security force ability to counter transnational organized crime. The MARFORSOUTH Security Cooperation Team is a small team of Marines from a variety of occupational specialties focused on developing, building and sustaining partnerships, and increasing regional stability through tailor-made training to fit the unique needs of partner nation forces.
  - ➢ Joint Riverine Training Teams (JRTT) composed of 10 to 15 personnel from the Marine Corps and Navy provided training support to partner nations. For approximately one month, the JRTT trained partner nation riverine and littoral security units, focusing on the interoperability of waterborne and ground units. Each JRTT team contains a task organized mix of occupational specialties tailored to the host nation requirements.
  - ➢ MARFORSOUTH employed Civil Affairs Teams in Belize and Honduras to develop partner nation ability to provide humanitarian assistance and disaster relief, and integrate appropriate government services in areas threatened by transnational organized crime. A Military Information Support Team in Colombia built the Colombian military's expertise and complemented Joint Interagency Task Force South's Operation MARTILLO by encouraging reports of illicit trafficking to appropriate authorities.
- **Southern Partnership Station – High Speed Vessel SWIFT 2013:** Southern Partnership Station (SPS) is a series of Navy/Marine Corps engagements that build partner capacity through subject matter expert exchanges with partner nation militaries and civilian security forces. SPS includes Community Relations Projects that focus on partnerships, shared interests, and shared values. A USMC detachment, embarked on HSV SWIFT, deployed to the USSOUTHCOM AOR February to May 2013 to conduct building partner capacity engagements in Belize, Guatemala, and Honduras.
- **Exercise TRADEWINDS:** TRADEWINDS is an exercise supporting the Caribbean Basin Security Initiative (CBSI) that facilitates cooperation to reduce illicit trafficking within the Caribbean. In 2013, MARFORSOUTH was Executive Planning Agent for

over 230 personnel from the U.S. Navy, Marine Corps, and Coast Guard, and 16 partner nations who exchanged knowledge and expertise in countering illicit trafficking, humanitarian assistance, disaster relief, and human rights. Due to funding reductions, the ground phase of TRADEWINDS was cancelled, but the Maritime Phase and the Senior Leaders Seminar were executed. The Maritime Phase, led by the U.S. Coast Guard, trained regional partner nations in maritime humanitarian assistance and counter-drug interdiction while the seminar consisted of table-top discussions on a Caribbean regional approach to countering drug trafficking in the Eastern Caribbean.

- **Exercise INTEGRATED ADVANCE:** MARFORSOUTH participated in Exercise INTEGRATED ADVANCE 2013, which examined a whole-of-government response to a Caribbean Mass Migration crisis. During this exercise, MARFORSOUTH augmented the 24 hour operations center with the U.S. Marine Corps (USMC) Crisis Augmentation Cell, increasing the ability of Commander, MARFORSOUTH, to command and control USMC forces in the AOR, and advising and ensuring the proper utilization of force by the ARSOUTH-led Joint Task Force.

- **Exercise NEW HORIZONS:** From June to September 2013, MARFORSOUTH provided rotations of Marine Reserve Combat Engineer Teams and Civil Affairs personnel in support of the U.S. Air Forces Southern NEW HORIZONS Humanitarian and Civic Assistance exercise. Over fifty USMC Reserve Marines conducted combat engineering/construction training in Belize supporting citizen safety and governance in under-governed areas of Belize.

- **Exercise UNITAS – Partnership of the Americas (POA):** This exercise enhances multinational operational readiness, interoperability, and security cooperation among U.S. and nine partner nation naval infantries. In 2012, the exercise focus was amphibious operations, and the demand for training in amphibious operations by Latin American navies continues to be strong. However, due to budget uncertainty, USSOUTHCOM cancelled the POA 2013 portion of Exercise UNITAS. POA 2014 is planned for execution in Chile.

Special Operations Command South
Headquarters: Homestead, Florida

- **Building Partner Capacity:** In 2013, SOCSOUTH maintained small elements in Guatemala, Honduras and El Salvador working with key units to improve ground and maritime interdiction, civil affairs, and intelligence capacities. In the Andean Ridge, SOCSOUTH partnered with Colombia and Peru to confront narco-terrorist insurgencies whose illicit trafficking operations extend throughout the hemisphere. Despite our fiscally constrained environment, SOCSOUTH used episodic engagements with key Southern Cone and Caribbean partners to facilitate relationships essential for maintaining future capacity building.

- **Civil Affairs:** In 2013, 11 civil affairs teams helped eight partner nations reduce the vulnerability of key populations intimidated by transnational organized crime or violent extremism. These teams assisted with counter-recruitment programs and, in many cases, helped partner nations build civil affairs capacities.

- **Information Operations:** SOCSOUTH maintained military information support teams (MIST) in seven key partner nations supporting the DOD Rewards Program, U.S. Government Anti-trafficking in Persons Program, partner nation counter-recruitment programs, and active tip lines in support of efforts against transnational organized criminal and violent extremist organizations. MISTs also conducted over 25 Subject Matter Expert Exchanges throughout the area of responsibility.

- **Intelligence Analytical Support to US Country Teams:** SOCSOUTH provides intelligence and counter-threat financing support to U.S. Country Teams focusing on terrorism, human smuggling networks, and transnational organized crime. In Colombia and Peru, SOCSOUTH helped develop host nation capabilities and country team support through a number of subject matter exchanges, and mentored them in institutionalizing intelligence pipelines.

- **Logistics Training and Advisory Team:** SOCSOUTH priority for building logistics capacity was in the Andean Ridge where they provided subject matter expertise to enable key Colombian partner units to establish a sustainable weapons-repair capability and initiate the development of an aerial delivery capability

- SOCSOUTH also assisted Peruvian units engaged in counter narco-terrorism operations in conducting a weapons inspection, which will serve as a starting point for future SOCSOUTH logistics engagement activities.

- **Building Intellectual Capital:** SOCSOUTH, in conjunction with the Colombian Joint Staff College, conducted a Counter-terrorism Fellowship Program-funded seminar in Bogota, Colombia, September 16-20, 2013. The event featured a cross-section of U.S. and Colombian subject matter experts and speakers, and included 70 participants from 12 countries in the Western Hemisphere

- **FUERZAS COMANDO 2013:** FUERZAS COMANDO 2013 was cancelled due to budget uncertainty.

- **FUSED RESPONSE 2013:** SOCSOUTH executes an annual CJCS-directed exercise to validate time sensitive crisis action planning, as well as training, readiness, interoperability and capability of Special Operations Forces in support of regional crises and contingencies. FUSED RESPONSE 2013 was a table-top exercise held at Homestead Air Reserve Base. It involved SOCSOUTH staff and lead planners from each of its components. The exercise focused on the areas of personnel planning, objectives development, and joint integration. Its aim was to improve the interoperability of the participant forces and increase the staff's capacity to confront common threats such as illicit traffic, organized crime, and terrorism.

Joint Task Force Guantanamo (JTF-GTMO)
Guantanamo Bay, Cuba

- **Safe and Humane Care and Custody:** JTF-GTMO conducted safe, humane, legal, and transparent care and custody of detainees, including those convicted by military commission. Detainees maintained family contact via mail, telephone calls and, in areas which support this service, videophone conferences coordinated by the International Committee of the Red Cross (ICRC). High quality Level II routine and urgent medical care was provided to detainees on a 24-hour basis. General surgical care, dental care, preventative medicine, optometry and mental health services were provided, or arranged, as was targeted specialty care on a recurring basis.

- **Legal and Transparent Operations:** Assessments of detention conditions by the ICRC continued with four visits in 2013. The ICRC verifies compliance with international standards of custody (as specified in the Geneva Conventions and other international standards) and provides confidential advice for suggested improvements to the Joint Task Force Commander and U.S. Southern Command. Detainees are granted routine visits by legal representatives, and received more than 1177 Military Commissions and 350 Habeas attorney visits in 2013. JTF-GTMO, committed to transparency, hosted 126 media representatives from 83 domestic and international news organizations; supported 77 visits with a combined total of 815 visitors; and answered hundreds of media queries during the past year.

- **Military Commissions:** Smooth execution of the Military Commissions process is another priority of JTF-GTMO. Military Commissions proceedings are open to observation by the media, victim family members, and non-governmental organizations. In 2013, JTF-GTMO supported eight hearings to address pre-trial motions of the five individuals accused of coordinating the September 11, 2001 attacks on the U.S. (referred to in the press as "the 9/11 Five"), and motion hearings for the alleged USS COLE bomber. Additionally, the court has entered a scheduling order, setting the trial for the alleged USS COLE bomber to commence on September 2, 2014.

Joint Interagency Task Force South (JIATF-S)
Key West, Florida

- **Joint Interagency Task Force South** contributed to the disruption of 132 metric tons of cocaine in FY2013, worth nearly $2.6 billion wholesale. JIATF-S employs an integrated defense forward capability for the ongoing efforts at the U.S. Southwest Border and for U.S. operations in the Western Hemisphere using tactical control (TACON) ship days, TACON flight hours, and the operating cost of Forces Surveillance Support Center relocatable over-the-horizon radar support.

- **The vast majority of JIATF-S successes came as a result of JIATF-S leadership and coordination of Operation (OP) MARTILLO,** the multi-lateral effects-based operation designed to deny the Central American littoral routes by illicit traffickers. Begun on January 15, 2012, OP MARTILLO to date results include the disruption of 272 metric tons of cocaine, the seizure of $10.7 million in bulk cash, and the seizure of 198 vessels and aircraft. Following its two year anniversary, OP MARTILLO is beginning to show its desired effects: trafficking in the Western Caribbean and Eastern Pacific littorals is decreasing while the activity in the Eastern Pacific non-littoral route is rising.

- **Operational Results and Impact:** In the air domain, over the past year, JIATF-S documented a 34 percent decrease in illicit air tracks destined for Central America (primarily Honduras). The illicit air corridor into Hispaniola was nearly absent during FY13 with only two flights documented moving into Haiti. In the maritime domain, during the same period, JIATF-S assessed a decrease of maritime activity in the Western Caribbean littoral and non-littoral trafficking areas of 43 percent and 45 percent for each vector respectively. In line with the goals of OP MARTILLO, JIATF-S recently documented a significant decrease in trafficking via "go fasts" boats using the littoral routes and, during the first month of FY14, an increase in go fasts bypassing the littoral routes in favor of more direct routes toward Honduras. JIATF-S continues to monitor this trend and hopes that recent success against go fasts employing these deeper routes does not push traffickers back to littoral routes. In the Eastern Pacific, the trafficking shows a steady decrease in the littorals (characterized by an overall increase of 71 percent at the end of FY12 to a 20 percent decrease in FY13), while the activity in the Eastern Pacific non-littorals appears to be increasing (from an increase of 12 percent in FY12 to an increase of 28 percent in FY13, including a recent increase in the use of routes South of the Galapagos). These changes are assessed to be a continued result of OP MARTILLO assets working in the littoral areas along the Guatemala/Mexico border, and may reflect the start of achieving the anticipated end result of the operation, driving the traffickers out of the littorals.

- **Supporting Defense of the Homeland.** Since its inception in September 2012, OP UNIFIED RESOLVE, the counter illicit trafficking operation supporting Puerto Rico, has substantially improved and formalized interoperability between JIATF-S, Coast Guard District 7, Coast Guard Sector San Juan, and the Customs and Border Protection (CBP) Office of Air and Marine Caribbean Air and Marine Branch in our shared Counter Illicit Trafficking operations in the following ways. Real time information sharing between JIATF-S and operational forces from USCG District 7, CBP's Caribbean Air and Marine Branch, and Coast Guard Sector San Juan has improved OP UNIFIED RESOLVE's effectiveness against secondary movements of cocaine to Puerto Rico from the primary Hispaniola corridor. This collaborative orchestration enhanced the effective sharing of resources in an austere operating environment. The maturity, strategic leadership, and tactical collaboration between JIATFS, the USCG, and CBP have greatly enhanced the effectiveness of countering illicit trafficking CIT operations in the Northeastern Caribbean.

- **Role of Partner Nations:** In FY 2013, 68 percent of JIATF-S disruptions were marked by partner nation participation. The role of our Latin American partners should not be understated. Of the 147 illicit trafficking events disrupted by JIATF-S in FY 2013, 74 of these (50 percent) would not have been successful without the support of our international partners. The existing and future contributions to the Transit Zone effort by the U.K., France, the Netherlands, and Canada continue to be significant and needed.

- **Information Dominance and Innovating to Meet Converging Threats:** JIATF-S continues to innovate in the face of asset reductions, and has developed several initiatives to enhance effectiveness and efficiency with the tools under their tactical control. JIATF-S is adept at Counter Threat Finance, tying the flow of illicit proceeds to the movement of drugs and other threat streams. The Container Cell Initiative is expanding the interdiction community's awareness of trafficking via commercial means, and their newest Network Discovery Initiative will gain insights into the highly connected and converging organizations at work in their JOA. For all of these reasons, JIATF-S remains at the forefront of supporting the delivery of focused success against transnational organized crime in the Western Hemisphere.

Joint Task Force Bravo (JTF-B)
Soto Cano Air Base, Honduras

- JTF-B supported Central American (CENTAM) countries in disrupting transnational organized crime by supporting the movement of partner nation law enforcement agencies and units in denying illicit airfields; destroying cash crops; disrupting lines of communication; providing medical evacuation support to partner nation military, law enforcement, and civilians; maintaining forward operating locations to stage and sustain Honduran and U.S. interagency operations; treating more than 8,243 medical patients, 1,754 dental patients, 1,052 immunizations, and 313 surgical patients; partnering with the Government of Honduras to build capacity for responding to natural and manmade disasters; and improving local firefighting capabilities.
- JTF-B supported the Honduran Army in destroying illicit airfields within the department of Gracias a Dios. JTF-B provided lift support for 6,350 lbs of demolitions to Forward Operating Location Mocoron for use by the Honduran 5th Infantry Battalion to crater 6 airfields being utilized by drug trafficking organizations.
- JTF-B supported the BDF by providing movement to 16 marijuana plantations for marijuana crop eradication. This assistance allowed the BDF to destroy 61,146 plants, 221 lbs of seeds, and 330 lbs processed marijuana, ultimately removing $12.5 million from the Belizean streets where Drug Trafficking Organizations would utilize the money to disrupt law and order in Belize.
- JTF-B provided air movement support to Homeland Security Investigations and Honduras Law Enforcement along the Honduran/Guatemalan border to disrupt illicit trafficking routes and enhance regional effects against Transnational Organized Crime operations.
- JTF-B conducts medical evacuation throughout Honduras. Over the past year, JTF-B provided 29 medical evacuation missions for 6 Honduran military members and 29 U.S. personnel.
- JTF-B conducted nine Medical Readiness Training Exercises (MEDRETEs) and Medical Surgical Teams (MSTs) (6 within Honduras, and 3 within CENTAM), as well as weekly MST missions to Santa Teresa Regional Hospital in Comayagua and a monthly trip to the Hospital Escuela in Tegucigalpa. Over the past year, JTF-B, with partner nation support, treated over 8,243 medical patients, 1,754 dental patients, 1,052 immunizations, and 313 surgical patients. The MEDRETEs and MSTs provide alternatives to transnational organized crime and gang patronage in isolated villages. Partner nation Military and Law Enforcement Agencies support the exercises, enabling interaction with isolated villages.
- JTF-B's CENTAM Survey and Assessment Team (C-SAT) provides a limited, but immediate, disaster response and relief capability within the region. It routinely integrates with the Government of Honduras in large-scale natural disaster exercises.

JTF-B also conducted their first multinational exercise in C-SAT history with several Belize government agencies and British forces, resulting in cooperative operations between C-SAT members, and an invite to Belize's hurricane planning conference.

- JTF-B supported more than a thousand children in several different orphanages, interacting with the children, donating much-needed supplies, and doing construction work on their buildings. For village support, JTF-B Chaplains organized 6 chapel hikes that donated and distributed 18,000 lbs of food, clothes, toys, and school supplies to approximately 3,900 community members. In October 2012, JTF-B partnered with the Se Pudo NGO to build 14 homes for families in 45 days, and, over the past year, participated in the Ajuterique Housing Project, which already helped construct 29 homes for families.

- JTF-B also provided critical support to Multi-national Search and Rescue Operations. JTF-B's unique capability to fly over water and provide recovery and extraction proved instrumental in the life-saving efforts of nine people lost at sea last July, including two U.S. personnel.